BROKEN CRAYONS STILL COLOR

Latoya Palmer

ISBN: 978-0-9983396-3-4

DEDICATION

I dedicate this book to my Mother, Father, Aunts, Uncles, Cousins, Sisters and Brothers. We survived the hand life dealt us. Now what will we do with the time we have left?

To Sharina Polk, Riana Robb, Falon Gibson, Jasamine Emanuel, Antwan Deligar, Derrian Mcgrew, Tearrieny Law, Tamika Stovall, Natasha Mckellum, and Alisia Johnson from Basic Training, to AIT, besties, war and the many different roles you've played in my life we made it out! Even if it was with scars, we're still breathing. I love you all! And I pray you collide with your destines.

To Melanie Frye-Cole, Apostle Cole, Cherisse Davenport, Ann Wilkerson, Belinda Wilkerson, Sophia Ruffin, First Lady Paulett Stone, and Pastor Kell Stone praying for me and loving me is an understatement. I pray that God pours back into you 100-fold what you have poured into me and so many others. And It is so In Jesus Name!

To my children T'kera and Christian I pray that the words I leave behind will help stir your ship away from some of the pain that I have endured. I pray that my journeys on this earth makes that much easier. I love you both to life and there is nothing you can do about it!

Latoya Palmer

Contents

Latoya Palmer

Broken Crayons Still Color

INTRODUCTION

Broken Crayons Still Color

When I was a little girl, I would watch my cousin RaChelle win all kinds of competitions, ribbons and trophies for coloring. I remember being so amazed at how well she could color. I tried to mimic her. Oftentimes, I would try to color with her crayons, but they would always break because I colored too heavy. RaChelle used all kinds of different techniques when she colored. She would outline the pictures and use tissue to smooth out the colors just to name a few. It was Awesome! My Aunt Darlene would buy new crayons for RaChelle because I broke them. I would ask for new crayons too, but she would always buy me the big crayons.

At the time, it made me feel special to have the big crayons, but when we got home, and I started to color, I quickly realized that I couldn't color the same way as I did before. I told my aunt that the big crayons must be broken because they didn't color. She explained that they weren't broken, they were special. And they would teach me to color without breaking, like the smaller crayons did. My cousin teased me and said that Special crayons are for Special people and that made me not want to use them anymore. So, later I went into RaChelle's room and stole her crayons and started to color with them. As I began to color, the crayons all broke as usual but this time I put them back in the box that they came from.

Aunt Darlene called me and said, "Latoya I'm going to punish you for breaking RaChelle's crayons!" I said, "How do you know that it was me, that broke the crayons?" She replied, "Because you are the only one that color hard enough to break them!" I asked my aunt to Please buy me some crayons like RaChelle's?" But she said, "No, you better color with the big crayons or use the little crayons that are already broken." That was the day that I realized, "Broken Crayons Still Color."

Caterpillars were born to fly but it doesn't mean that they were born knowing it. Sometimes you must discover your wings, before you can ever begin to fly. God created you and I with purpose, but some of us still haven't learned to fly. The day that you discover your wings, will also be the day that you take flight!

Beautifully Broken

Remember that the mind is also the

battleground

and if the enemy gets your mind he

already has you.

I've spent my whole life searching

for something that seemed unattainable

and ultimately outside of my reach,

but then I was introduced to God

who showed me that ALL things are

possible

and NO GOOD THING would he

withhold from me.

If I would delight myself in the Lord,

He would give me the desires of my

heart.

And although every day is not a bed of

roses,

And I don't cross every "T" nor do I dot

every " i ",

I strive to be the difference that I want

to see in this world.

Sometimes the burden seems too hard

to bear and it seems as if I have already

cried a river. But when I'm done, and before I lay my head to the pillow to rest, I somehow find my smile and give it to God. Because the world will never make me rob him of that.

I did not expect God's Grace, but now I must open myself to the pain of it, to feel the joy of it!

The Cost

The oil cost me

It cost me more than I wanted to pay

The oil cost me

Many days I saw my grave

The oil cost me

It cost me "my friends"

The oil cost me

It cost me "my love"

The oil cost me

It cost me "my life"

I promise you this oil has a cost

You see my anointing, I see my cross
You see my gain, I see my loss
You see my strengths, but I see you
asking for the cross
Do you see the work, because I've
counted the cost
I've saved all the receipts, because of
the cost
Just like your oil will cost you
There was a funeral held, on the same
day that I was born
I guess that's why they say with every
death, new life is formed
Now for all who were or were not in
attendance; let me tell you who you've

lost

You've lost the girl that was a slave to sin

Bound in her own mind and limited by

her own choices

You lost the promises she made to hold

you down

When she couldn't even hold herself up

You lost the loyalty she gave you

While everyday being disloyal to herself

You lost the right to hold her

Bound to promises made as an

incomplete person

You lost the right to tell her what she

owes you

and that you remember what she did

You lost the right to tell her from where

she came

And who she'd be

You lost the girl with no "heart"

The heartless girl, because she gave

away every part of her heart to thee

Leaving nothing for the creator

The healer of all things

So here I am to tell you this; her last

request

to read her final wishes

Her Life's Will reads as this:

To every one of you, I Leave nothing,

but a slate wiped clean, just as Christ

did for me that day on Calvary. There is no need for tears and sorry. My death is not the end. I was born the day I died, to live this life again.

2 Corinthians 12:9 KJV

My grace is sufficient for thee: for my strength is made perfect in weakness.

Guess what?

Guess what?

We are all Human

Yep, just Human

But, yet we are spirit

they've got skin

You've got skin,

And I've got skin

We've got skin for days

We're easily Broken, scarred, and

bruised

Many have become numb to the pain
How do I know, because I've been there
too
So much has happened until you
catapult through
No more living; just existing
No more thriving; merely surviving
But that's not spiritual strength; that's
spiritual weakness
What if I tell you it's a false hood
The definition of natural strength that
the world has taught us; just always
surviving
Merely a trick and a trap of the enemy
True strength is to endure the

unendurable and allow it to spill over

into joy

All while giving glory and honor to God

Now that's strength!

It behooves us to teach people everything we know, because we never know when our next level, breakthrough, or even our very existence is contingent upon what we've taught.

I Failed You

I failed you my daughter

My beauty, my queen

I failed you my daughter

Before you had wings

I Crippled your mind and stunted your growth

I left you in the hands of those

That never allowed me to grow

I failed you my daughter

My beauty, my queen

I failed you my daughter

Latoya Palmer

Before you had wings

Now I'm here picking up the pieces

Broken, discarded, forgotten pieces

A puzzle piece here, a puzzle piece there

And you wonder why the picture

that you're looking at isn't clear, but

your vision's distorted

And every pair of bifocals you pick up

have frames but no lens

God gave you a pair that were ever so

clear

but because you no longer like the

frames

you sat them on the chair

You talked about them

And allowed others to do the same

not realizing that one day, God would

use those glasses

to give sight to all that have been blind

I failed you my daughter

My beauty, my queen

I failed you my daughter

Before you had wings.

Luke 4:18 (KJV)

18 The Spirit of the Lord is upon me,
because he hath anointed me to preach
the gospel to the poor; he hath sent me
to heal the brokenhearted, to preach
deliverance to the captives, and
recovering of sight to the blind, to set at
liberty them that are bruised,

I Can't Save You

I can't save you

My tears want me to run to you

But I can't save you

My heart wants me to help you through

But, we both know; that I can't save

you

I can't save you, from yourself

I can't save you cause at night you

sleep with you alone

Wake up to you, Talk to you

How can I save you when 90% of your
time is spent alone with you
You only come to me like a junkie for a
fix
When you want to escape the barriers
of your mind
That you alone can't fix
When you can't swallow the tears no
more
When the girls and boys don't satisfy
you inside your core
Now you come to me with either that
text or that call
But it's always that same reply.... Hey
And if it's been a long time you'll even

add.... "Hey Stranger" to the mix

But truth be told I never left

I'm the one you dissed

You should break up with yourself from time to time

Because you listen to you more than the creator speaking inside

Oh, did you forget about him, the one that made you

Yeah, now you get the picture of why I can't save you

I would be doing Christ Job and we both know I'm not Abel,

Yea you know the one that was killed at the hands of his brother

Cause that's what I would be doing if I

don't lead you to the Father

Killing you daily just not because you

had the better offering

So, my tears may fall, and my heart

may break

But every time you call, I'll point you to

Christ face

Not to His hand but to the Master's face

He wants to heal you, but you must be

willing

Death is sweeping, it is sweeping

through the city

Picking up God's people that have

finished their course

But also picking up the ones that.

couldn't make the choice

If you can't be used for God's glory;

then why are you here

Christ is coming for His bride

Will you be ready or not

Like a builder building a house, will you

be the brick, mortar, cornerstone,

wood or maybe a beam

Or will you be the saw dust that fell to

the ground

Cause death is sweeping through and its

leaving no stone unturned.

Don't throw in the towel, refold it with Faith!

Jesus Saves!!!!!!!

Latoya Palmer

Deep

There was this part of me that was so

dark and sinister

No matter how I tried to hide it

to cover it up

to bury it sometimes

I heard her speak

It was a lowly voice saying let me out

I just want to play

Tears filled the back of my eyes because

I remembered her

And if I'm honest she is who I knew

I didn't know the new Toya that I was

becoming

just like you, I was meeting her too

I loved my past and I embraced it

because it gave me a sense of worth

and control

No one could take it away or change it

Or tell me that it didn't happen

I lived it

Latoya Palmer

I owned it

It was me without apology

I was lost without words

thoughts clouded my mind of what to

do next

every step was truly taken blindly

Somedays I woke up hoping someone

would call with a plan

because I did not have one

Or they would just simply hold my hand

Dysfunction was better than no function

I could work with chaos because it was

better than the sound of silence

Especially when you were lost

I think I helped people, so I didn't have

to save myself

That was truly the hardest journey of

my life

saving that little girl from herself.

I told Her

I struggle sometimes with giving my

daughter the truth

without photoshop.

I mean that ugly unadulterated truth,

Not fixed up with comfort and pretty

words.

But tonight, was different and without

apology.

Truth in living color,

with tears raging down my face I told

her how selfish she is.

I told her....

Forgive People for not being what you

expected them to be.

Restoration

There is a demon, his name is silence

And he's coming for you

He's shutting your mouths and you have
no clue

He is deceitful, treacherous, unfaithful,
dangerous and traitorous too

He will go after your children, if he can't
get you

Silence is deadly, and he is choking the life out you

Christ is the giver of life

He spoke it forth

From, let there be light; to the creation of Adam

He used his word

Gave Adam authority to name everything in the world

But lonely is how God saw him, so he gave him a queen

Don't get it twisted there is a time for

silence in everything,

but not in the things that are keeping

you in bondage

Eves mistake was taking advice from the

one with no authority

And now the very people that are made

in his image to speak

and help produce life,

are allowing the demon of silence to

run ramped in their life

Angry with your daughters when she
wouldn't make a peep
but how many family secrets did you
keep under the cover
too afraid to speak
Or did you allow them to keep you in
bondage too afraid to come up for air
God made Adam and Eve not Adam and
Steve
That has become the argument
But you must understand,

Adam and Eve were born from the

Genesis

There was no sin found within,

but everything that came after was born

in sin and shaped in inequity

God's perfection became man's

imperfection

The sin filled breed

On their way to eternal damnation

But

God stepped in

Bringing man restoration

Love is a debt that you will never pay off. You will always be in debt to love.

If God answered the prayers you prayed today, would someone else's life or just your life be changed?

Freedom

When sin demanded justice for my soul

Grace and Mercy said, "Oh……No

We already paid the price.

So, I'm standing here with a receipt in

hand

saying paid in full for the sin I never

paid.

So, today and every day I die for the

man from Galilee

who once stood in my stead.

They hung him high

they stretched him wide,

He hung his head, for me He died.

Crown of thorns on his head for me,

stabbed and ridiculed for me,

spat in face for me,

beaten and bruised just for me,

whipped, cracked back for me.

And here I stand afraid to live the life

He died to give.

John 3:16 King James Version

(KJV)

16 For God so loved the world, that he
gave his only begotten Son, that
whosoever believeth in him should not
perish, but have everlasting life.

Where'd the Time Go

Where'd the time go

Yesterday you were just a babe

Where'd the time go,

You're almost grown

Where'd the time go

I remember holding you in my arms

Now, you're always on my heart

Man, Where'd the time go my love

Time waits for no one

Latoya Palmer

Not you, Not me

It just rolls right along

So, hug as much as possible

And give as much as you can

People need you

I need you

Even when our worlds change

I'll pray for you daily

Just as I always have

But stop saying

You're okay when you're not

Before I'm gone, and the world believes you

Ecclesiastes 3 King James Version

(KJV)

3 To everything there is a season, and a
time to every purpose under the
heaven:

Spiritual Father

Drowning in thoughts

Lost for words

You called me daughter

I called you Father

But, I didn't know the meaning of the word.

God lead me to you

And in my heart, it was true

But where do I start loving a man

When I didn't even know how to love the man

Whose loins I came through

Loving his wife as a mother was easy

Because she was so different

God wanted to fulfil His promise

But I had to be willing

Willing to travel this road

A road never paved

Proverbs 13:1 (MSG)

Intelligent children listen to their parents; foolish children do their own thing.

God's (But Your Mine)

The enemy is tricking you

Deceiving you like he did Adam, Eve and

the serpent too

Your falling for the lies

A slave to compromise

He's got a spell on you

(But your Mine)

Men Wearing Dresses

Women pimping and sagging

Everyone switching places

Spell bound; the whole race

Your falling for the lies

A slave to compromise

He's got a spell on you

(But your mine)

You killed the boy you once were

You've slain the girl you once loved

all because the world

Made you question who you really were

But it didn't stop there, it gets much

worst

The rest of the world is confused too

and forgotten who they were too

The trans be popping

Doing extra to be you

That you start doing extra to compete

with them

And forget how to be you

And because you forgot you

Men forgot you too

And can see no difference between the

Tran

And the woman in you

Your falling for the lies

A slave to compromise

He’s got a spell on you

(But your mine.)

Jeremiah 29:11

For I know the thoughts that I think toward you, saith the LORD, thoughts of peace, and not of evil, to give you an expected end.

Latoya Palmer

ME

Angry at life

Angry at you
Questioning everyone else

instead of questioning you

Why did he leave,

why did she stay

Not realizing that everyone makes

Mistakes

Angry at life

Mad at you

Questioning everyone,

instead of you

It doesn't matter who left

It doesn't matter who stayed

What matters is that you change your

flip flopping ways

When you make a mistake

you blame it on them

They didn't teach you and they didn't

show you the way

but truth be told you're blaming without

all the facts

In math an equation cannot be solved

if not the right amount of information is

involved

X+Y= 20 can be solved, but it's hard

because there are many Scenarios that

can get you here

Now X+140-34=Y; you can't solve

because not enough information is

involved

So, stop looking at people and thinking

that they owe you

or failed you when you never asked

them who they are

You are them

the epitome of what you hate

so, stop blaming others yet forgiving

yourself

Because Him+Her=You

and Her-Him subtracts you too

So, learn to add using our savior.

Because him+her^by the savior=you

as God created

People are flawed; some broken and

empty vessels

So how do you propose a broken glass

holds water

You are a rose; beautiful indeed, but

roses have thorns the only protection

they need

So, your thorns represented God who's

also the living water

Now that's all that you require

So instead, you’re depending on a

broken glass that can't even hold water

If touched wrong, can even cut you

Stand on the creator

He'll heal your hurt and help you find

the you,

that you've even hidden from yourself

Mad at people because they call you a

flip flopper;

but aren't you

Most people see what you show them

But you try so hard to cover up what's

inside that it makes you unstable

You know who you were

but don't see who you've become.

Peace is not a Destination, it is a Journey!

<u>A Slave to Sin</u>

A Slave to Sin

I was in

No holds barred

I gave it my all

Lost never to be found

Bound and chained

To a life I made

Cuffs on hands

Chains on feet

Walking around on a leash

Sin was walking me

But I thought I was walking it

On all fours; a dog in the spirit

Loyal to any and everything Satan sent.

Sometimes things have to come end;

your favorite movie, song, and

sometimes your favorite book, it's just

life.

Pinocchio

There's a lump in my throat

Words choke

Smoke and mirrors

The devils cloak

Eyes open wide shut

You refuse to believe

Yet you claim to love me

All along, a puppet in this rat race

Your Mother's a modern day Geppetto

So, I guess that makes you Pinocchio

Latoya Palmer

A liar in your own right

A master of disguise

So, tell me are you the toy or are you

the girl

Because you play too many games

you are telling me one thing

but every day I see your NOSE change

In my face when it's convenient

But in your mothers when you are

feigning

Feigning for the boys for the drinks and

for the drugs

But it's over.... Pinocchio

It's over because

when I thought you were a girl

I prayed for you

I cried for you

Stayed up late nights petitioning God for you

But you turned like a dog going back to his vomit

It's true

I cannot stand here and wait on you

I have two children that I've been petitioning God for too

And I must do what I must do

So, in the back of my mind I'll whisper a

silent prayer for you

And pray that you find your way and

accept God's grace because it is

sufficient for you

And just like Pinocchio maybe one day

you will be real too

Real… It cannot be taught, bought,

imitated, manufactured, created,

manipulated, or duplicated

You just are or you’re not

Mankind

The (wo)man with no Heart

My Grandmother told me many moons ago

That the heart is truly sacred

It's two sided and untamed without the Creator

She said the heart is a wild animal

That's why our ribs are caged

Deceitfully wicked, it truly is

That's why God judges the heart of a (wo)man

The human eye can't see it or begin to understand

What's hidden behind its many layers in
the body
one of the 3 things God caged
The heart is fragile and needs
protection from itself
The same God that didn't cage wild
animals
caged your heart, brain and lungs
When God blew the ruah breath of life
in you
He blew it in those very lungs giving you
two
Because He knew it would
be difficult for you to breathe
With just you

The simplest things complicate the most sophisticated minds.

There's more to my story than what

they said!

25559994R00050

Made in the USA
Columbia, SC
05 September 2018